The Little Book of JavaScript

The Little Book of JavaScript

Karl Agius

2014

First Printing: 2014

ISBN 978-1-312-46602-9

http://karlagius.com

About this book

It has been almost two decades since I first taught myself JavaScript, mostly by reading through the source on any internet page which struck me as interesting. The language, and the industry's attitude to it, has changed significantly in this span of time.

From a 'toy' language used to open annoying popups and changing the colour of things, JavaScript is now being used to build substantial, even mission critical applications. With Node.js, it is even finding its way onto the server side, which can only be described as an excellent thing.

JavaScript skills are valuable, and given the direction that the industry is headed in, one can assume that they're going to become more so in time. However, there seems to be a knowledge gap which I often encounter when working with new developers who have only been exposed to JavaScript through the filter of a framework. A gap which sometimes leaves them stuck or confused as they are missing some concepts which the framework designers reasonably assumed they would know.

The frameworks and tools available today are fantastic in terms of getting things done. Speaking for myself, I don't think I've written any non-trivial applications without using a framework in ages, and I am certainly not advocating getting rid of them. On the contrary, I believe that understanding what goes on beneath the frameworks helps coders get more power out of them.

This book is for average developers who already have some knowledge of coding, but little experience in using raw JavaScript. Old hands – anyone who's been exposed to the language before jQuery and other frameworks burst onto the scene – will most likely know most of the things described here inside out.

For everyone else, I hope that the information presented here will prove useful in your projects.

Table of Contents

Some basics

To begin with, we are going to go over some very basic concepts. Chances are that you've already used most of them at some point, perhaps without even knowing it. Or maybe you're aware of them but not in depth.

Either way we're going to take a closer look at them, because while they look simple, there's the scope for them to cause all kinds of shenanigans by stopping your scripts from working (bad) or making your scripts work almost, but not quite, the way you intended (much, much worse).

Variable definition

Unlike many languages, JavaScript doesn't force you to declare your variables beforehand, and will implicitly initialise them the first time they are used[1].

You can, however, explicitly initialise them by using the var keyword, for example

```
var a = 10;
```

In some cases, this will not make much of a difference. However, implicit declaration may have some unpleasant side effects when you start to work with multiple scopes – think of implicit assignment as way of saying "ok, make a new variable if it doesn't exist already, but if you have one with the same name, chuck out whatever is in it and replace it". That is almost never going to be what you want it to do.

---

[1] This changes if strict mode is enabled, but we won't worry about that for now.

Undefined variables

Variables which have not been defined or initialised are in an undefined state. Calling typeof on such variables will return the result of "undefined". You can use this to test whether a variable is defined or otherwise:

```
if (typeof(a) == "undefined")
```

Note that undefined and null are different. A variable that has a null value has been set explicitly; you are saying "This thing has a null value". An undefined value means "I have no idea what this thing is, yet".

In some cases, you can also use the not operator (!) to determine if something is undefined:

```
if (!a)
```

However, this will not give you the same results as typeof.

If a is undefined or has been set to null, !a will resolve to true, but the check with typeof will return false if the value is set to null – again, because null is not undefined. In general, the not operator is enough if you need to check for a usable value, except in two cases: Boolean or numeric values.

With Booleans, the problem is simple – false is a definite value, and we don't want to assume that that is undefined. With numbers, the situation is slightly greyer. JavaScript treats the numeric value of 0 as a Boolean false, and any non-zero value as a Boolean true. Since 0 may well be a valid, usable value, it is better to test using the typeof check.

Strict and Lenient Equality

When it comes to comparing things, JavaScript offers two operators – lenient equality (==), which you will almost certainly have come across, and its slightly less famous sibling, strict equality (===).

The lenient equality operator tests whether the values between two variables are the same. It returns true if the values are equivalent – that is, if the values can be converted to a common type and their values are equal. So

```
"10" == 10
```

would evaluate to true even if one is a string and the other is a number, because the values are the same – 10. On the other hand,

```
"10" === 10
```

will evaluate to false, because the types are different. For Java and .Net developers, it's worth noting that

```
10.0 === 10
```

Will still evaluate to true, as they are both of the type number – JavaScript does not have different types for fractional numbers.

Neither strict nor lenient equality will return true when you are comparing complex objects. This is because you would be comparing the references to the objects, not the values inside them. This would always evaluate to false unless you are comparing exactly the same instance of an object.

Logical and Bitwise operators

Again, Boolean operators are so ubiquitous that anyone who has been doing coding for any amount of time will be familiar with them. We are just going to go over them very quickly for sake of completeness.

And: & and &&

The logical "and" operator can be used to compare two expressions and will return true if both are true. The most commonly used form is the short-circuit and (&&) – this form will only evaluate the second expression if the first one is true. Since both of them need to be true anyway, if the first one is false then there's no point in trying to evaluate the second one.

For this reason, you should always put the most trivial checks first. In other words, if in the following examples fastFunction returns false and slowFunction returns true:

```
var state = (slowFunction() && fastFunction());
```

will perform more slowly than

```
var state = (fastFunction() && slowFunction());
```

because the first expression will always be evaluated. The second expression is only evaluated if the first one is true. In the examples above, you can see that the first version would always

[7]

run the slow function, while the second one only runs the slow function if the fast function evaluates to true. In other words, it only does the slow stuff if it absolutely has to, which is what we want.

A word of caution; be careful when your operation involves two functions which have secondary effects – changing some values, for example. Since the second expression isn't guaranteed to run, you cannot assume that it will be. In general, it is a good design practice to separate the code which checks stuff and the code which does stuff.

The bitwise and operator (&) is slightly less common but fulfils more or less the same tasks, with some variations.

The most obvious difference is that this operator will always execute both expressions, regardless of the result of the first one (assuming that it does not throw an exception, of course). So in this case, there is no difference between the following two lines:

```
var state = (slowFunction() & fastFunction());
var state = (fastFunction() & slowFunction());
```

because both functions will always be executed anyway. For this reason, it is almost always better to use the short circuit operator, as it saves some processing time.

Another, slightly more subtle difference is that the bitwise operator will return 1 (for true) and 0 (for false) rather than an actual Boolean value. In most cases, this makes absolutely no difference, since JavaScript can interpret those two values as true or false anyway.

The real use for the bitwise operator is to make bit comparisons.

For example, "2 & 3" will return 2. This is the result of the shared bits between the two numbers being returned. Taking the binary representations:

	32	16	8	4	2	1
2	0	0	0	0	1	0
3	0	0	0	0	1	1
&	0	0	0	0	1	0

The bit they share in common is the second one, which can be translated back into a 2. Taking some larger numbers, say 28 and 15:

	32	16	8	4	2	1
28	0	1	1	1	0	0
15	0	0	1	1	1	0
&	0	0	1	1	0	0

28 and 15 share bits 8 and 4, so 28 & 15 gives us 12.

Or: | and ||

The same points apply for the "or" logical operators. The short circuit operator (||) will only evaluate the second expression if the first one evaluates to false – since it will return true if either of the two expressions is true, it doesn't need to check the second one if the first one was true.

The bitwise operator (|) can be used to determine which bits are in either of the two values. So for 2 | 3 we expect to get a 3:

	32	16	8	4	2	1
2	0	0	0	0	1	0
3	0	0	0	0	1	1
|	0	0	0	0	1	1

While 28 | 15 will give us 31:

	32	16	8	4	2	1
28	0	1	1	1	0	0
15	0	0	1	1	1	0
|	0	1	1	1	1	0

The Negation Operator

The negation operator (!) is thankfully much more straightforward. If the expression evaluates to true, it will return false, and vice versa. Nothing else to see here.

The Ternary Operator

In my personal opinion, this operator is criminally underused. It can be used as shorthand for an if-else condition to set a variable.

```
var message = (!name)
    ? "No name given"
    : "Hello " + name;
```

This reads "Declare a variable called message. If name is not defined, set message to 'no name given', otherwise set it to 'hello' + name".

While I know that some people prefer to avoid the ternary operator due to readability concerns, I feel that it's just as easy to read in this form as it is in the longer form.

Scopes

In any piece of code, everything exists inside a scope. You can think of scopes as rooms with all your items in them. In general, you can only access items which were defined in your current scope, or in a parent scope (more on that later).

In JavaScript it's particularly important to be aware of the current scope, since touching an item outside your current scope may not necessarily result in an error. This can often lead to some unusual and definitely undesirable behaviour.

Scopes are delimited by functions. Basically, anything declared inside a function can only be seen within that function. For example:

```javascript
var externalVariable =
"This string exists in this scope, and any nested
scope.";

function internal() {
    var internalVariable =
        "This string only exists inside this scope";

    console.log("Scope 2: " + externalVariable);
    console.log("Scope 2: " + internalVariable);
}

internal();

console.log("Scope 1: " + externalVariable);
console.log("Scope 1: " + internalVariable);
```

This would cause an error on the last line, because internalVariable only exists within the scope of the internal function.

This only affects variable definitions, **not** the values inside variables. If you change the value of an external variable within a scope, the new value will be used wherever your variable can be used. For example:

```
var externalVariable = "My initial value";

function internal() {
    externalVariable = "I got modified";
}

internal();
console.log(externalVariable);
```

In this case, the output will be "I got modified", because we changed the value of an existing variable.

Within the same function, variables which are defined inside a code block (for example a condition) remained defined even after you leave that code block. For example,

```
if (x < 1) {
    var message = "Hi!";
}

console.log(message);
```

[13]

will result in "Hi!" if the condition is true, or "Undefined" if the condition evaluates to false. This is different from the way scopes work in other languages, where scopes are delimited by code blocks.

While this behaviour lets you define variables inside a code block, it does not follow that you should do this, as it can lead to confusion. This also applies to variables and iterators in for loops – the variable will remain defined outside the loop with the last value it was assigned. If you love crawling through code with a debugger, go ahead and use this. For the rest of us however, it's best avoided.

Redefining variables in a scope

To avoid accidentally overwriting the value of a variable in an external scope, it's a good idea to explicitly declare that you are initializing a new variable by using the var keyword. This allows you to preserve the value of the variable:

```javascript
var myNiceText = "My initial value";

function internal() {
    var myNiceText = "A different value";
    console.log("Scope 2: " + myNiceText);
}

internal();
console.log("Scope 1: " + myNiceText);
```

The output for this will be:

```
Scope 2: A different value
Scope 1: My initial value
```

The difference between this example and the previous one is the use of the var keyword. By specifying this keyword, we are stating that we want to initialize a new variable in the current scope, and store this value in it, leaving the variable with the same name in the external scope untouched.

In general, you would do well to avoid having different variables in different scopes using the same name, as doing so will almost inevitably result in confusion.

Closures

The rules for scopes are very slightly different when we are returning a function from another function, like so:

```
function myFunction(text) {

    var prefix = text;

    return function(name) {
            console.log(prefix + " " + name);
    }
}

var action = myFunction("Hello");
action("World");
action("Karl");
```

In this case, we are creating a second function inside the first one, which references the variable called prefix. Since the function was created within the scope of the first function, it retains a reference to that scope. In this way, the prefix remains available to the second function, allowing it to output

```
Hello World
Hello Karl
```

This is called a closure; we will return to it later when we discuss functions, but for now it is enough that you understand the effect on the scope.

Functions

Functions are vital in JavaScript. While they're not the smallest unit of code you can use, it's unlikely that you will ever write any significant scripts without using them. If you have, please get off that unicorn now.

The idea is to use functions to group statements together so you have a reusable, isolated behaviour. Once your function is defined, you can execute it any number of times without having to repeat all those statements each time.

Working in any other way would quickly get out of hand once you set your sights higher than a "Hello world" script, so let's see how we can make functions work for us.

Declaring functions

Functions may be declared in three ways. The most common way is the following:

```
function myAction() {
        console.log("O Hai!");
}
```

In this case, you are declaring a function called myAction in the current scope, which can then be called as follows:

```
myAction();
```

When you see the name of a function followed by brackets, that is a function call – we are telling it to do something. If there are no brackets, it's a function reference – we're going to do something with it.

The second way is to use the same notation as you would for a variable declaration:

```
var myAction = function() {
        console.log("O Hai!");
}
```

This is functionally (yeah. Sorry.) identical to the previous form.

In both cases, the function is declared within the current scope. If you declare this in the global scope, it is accessible anywhere, while if you declare it inside a function, it is only accessible inside that function. It is no different in this respect than any other variable.

Less common is the Function constructor, which allows you to generate functions from strings. This may seem like a great idea if you really need the added flexibility, but you really need to be careful as you can introduce all sorts of logical problems in your script. To create a new function in this way, you can use:

```
var myAction = new Function("console.log('O
Hai!')");
```

This is mostly identical to the previous two examples, except that functions created in this manner do not use closures.

When you are working with strings you may run into problems with quoted values. Above, we used single quotes to define a string inside another delimited by double quotes. Another way to do this is to escape the quote characters, like so:

```
var myAction = new Function("console.log(\"O
Hai!\")");
```

The slash tells the script that the quote right after it is just part of the text, and should not close the string.

[19]

Function parameters

The function we declared in the previous section does one thing only – it logs "O Hai!" every time that is called. Not exactly what one might call useful.

In most cases, we will want our functions to be a bit more versatile. This would usually mean that we need to give them more information. Of course we could dump all our possible variables in the global scope and let all the functions access them, but that would be terrible to manage unless you're writing something really quick and dirty[2].

A much cleaner solution is to use parameters to pass information into the function, for example:

```
function square(value) {
        console.log(value * value);
}
```

We can then call this function by passing in any value we want when we want it:

```
square(2);
```

---

[2] From experience, even quick and dirty scripts seem to have this tendency to ... grow. It's often a terrifying experience to rediscover a "temporary" script one has written years back.

The value parameter will be treated as a variable that only exists inside this function.

Since JavaScript does not support function overloading, we cannot declare different functions with different sets or different types of parameters.

However, it's not very picky when it comes to accepting parameters. We could, for example, call the square function we just wrote above with one, two or really any number of parameters.

Of course in this case only one parameter would actually be used, but we could easily script functions to work with optional parameters:

```javascript
function describe(thing, adjective) {

    var message = "This is a " + thing + ". ";

    if (adjective)
          message = message + adjective + ", don't
you think?";

    console.log(message);
};

describe("Callahan fullbore autolock");
describe("hat", "Pretty cunning");
```

In the first call, we're only passing in one parameter; the adjective argument[3] remains undefined, so the condition evaluates to false and only the first part of the message is logged:

```
This is a Callahan fullbore autolock.
```

In the second case, adjective is defined, so the second part of the message is added on:

```
This is a hat. Pretty cunning, don't you think?
```

You can easily extend this to handle more optional parameters, although if they start increasing in number, it might be a sign that you're putting way too much in a single function.

If you are using the function constructor for your function, you can declare parameters by passing them in before your function body, like so:

```
var describe = new Function("thing",
"console.log(\"This is a \" + thing + \".\")");
```

Any number of parameters can be declared in this way; the last argument you pass to the function constructor will be used as the function code.

---

[3] Parameters are the names you declare when you are declare a function. Arguments are the actual values you pass in when you call it.

Value and reference arguments

When you pass an argument of a primitive type (string, number etc) into a function, the function receives a copy of the value. Any changes to the argument will be available within the function, but the original variable is not affected. For example

```
var change = function(val) {
    val = val + "_changed";
    console.log("Inside: " + val);
}

var value = "a";
change(value);
console.log("Outside: " + value);
```

The output will be

```
Inside: a_changed
Outside: a
```

The value of the original has been preserved outside the function. We call this passing arguments "by value".

By contrast, if an argument is an object type, any changes to values inside it will be reflected outside the function. This is because when we pass in an object, we are giving the function a copy of the reference to an object, rather than a copy of the value. The copy of the reference will still point to the original, so that gets changed:

```
var change = function(obj) {
    obj.value = obj.value + "_changed";
    console.log("Inside: " + obj.value);
}

var obj = { value: "a" };
change(obj);
console.log("Outside: " + obj.value);
```

Will result in

```
Inside: a_changed
Outside: a_changed
```

We call this passing arguments by reference.

Note that this only applies to changes made to values inside objects, rather than objects themselves. Since object is in itself a primitive type, if we change an entire object (rather than its properties) then the original object will not be affected since we are changing the reference. So:

```
var change = function(obj) {
    obj = { value: "new stuff!" }
    console.log("Inside: " + obj.value);
}

var obj = { value: "a" };
change(obj);
console.log("Outside: " + obj.value);
```

[24]

Will give us

```
Inside: new stuff!
Outside: a
```

Return values

Now, in most cases you will want to use several functions together, so you can do some complex processing without having massively overcomplicated functions[4].

You will want to pass the result of one function to the outside, so you can do something else with it. This is done using the return keyword:

```
var square = function(number) {
    return number * number;
}

var result = square(3);
console.log(result);
```

This will log "9". The return keyword takes the value it is given (in this case, the result of number * number) and passes it out of the function, in this case assigning it to the result variable.

Once the return statement is hit, your function will exit immediately, and any code after it will be ignored. For example:

---

[4] The "separation of concerns" design principle suggests that each function should do one thing and one thing only. While you may sometimes have to cram more stuff into a function, in general this is a good principle to follow as it gives you smaller, easier to understand functions which are more reusable.

```
var square = function(number) {
    var result = number * number;
    return result;
    console.log("The result is: " + result);
}
```

In this case, the log function will never be called because it occurs after the return statement.

You can of course have multiple return statements in your function as long as they represent different code paths (for example, different branches of an if statement):

```
var speak = function(type) {

    if (type === "dog")
        return "woof";

    if (type === "sheep")
        return "baaa";

    if (type === "cow")
        return "moo";
}
```

Opinion is divided on whether or not you should use multiple return statements. Some people hold that having multiple exit points can make the code confusing.

My personal opinion is that multiple exit points can make the code cleaner as you do not need to use as many else statements – in the example above, we do not need to use "else" since the function will exit as soon as it finds the first matching condition anyway. You may want to experiment with this and find the approach which you prefer.

Functions do not need to have a return value, and if they do, not all code paths need return a value. In the example above, if none of the conditions match, the function will simply return nothing. In this case, the return value would be undefined.

You can also call the return statement with no value:

```
return;
```

When this statement is hit, the function will exit immediately with an undefined return value.

Fluent APIs

Some APIs, like jQuery, allow you to chain functions together to create a more readable sequence of actions. This kind of API is called fluent, and is usually implemented by having each function return an object which defines further functions which can be called. In many cases this will be the same instance object on which the first function was called, but it may be a different object entirely.

```
var MyMath = function(number){

    var self = this;
    this.innerNumber = number;

    this.add = function(number) {
            self.innerNumber += number;
            return self;
    };

    this.subtract = function(number) {
            self.innerNumber -= number;
            return self;
    };

    this.result = function() {
            return self.innerNumber;
    };
};

var math = new MyMath(1);
var result = math.add(5).subtract(2).result();

console.log(result);
```

In the example above, the add and subtract functions return the math instance as their return value, instead of the result of their operation. This allows us to chain calls together, which would result in a more readable line of code.

[29]

Functions as variables

Unlike methods in Java or .net, functions are treated as first class objects in JavaScript. This means that you can pass them around and manipulate them in much the same way you could a string or a number.

You will almost certainly have made use of this feature if you have spent any time at all using any framework – it is used extensively to provide callbacks to asynchronous functions or to 'smart' parameters.

```javascript
var calculateCostOnWeight = function(data) {
    return data.weight * 0.2;
}

var calculateTax = function(data) {
    return data.price * 0.15;
}

var calculateTotalCost = function(item,
additionalCosts) {
    var price = item.price;
    for (var index in additionalCosts)
            price += additionalCosts[index](item);

    return price;
}

var item = { price: 10.00, weight: 1.00 }
var totalCost = calculateTotalCost(
    item, [calculateCostOnWeight, calculateTax]);
```

```
console.log(totalCost);
```

In this example, we have defined two functions (calculateCostOnWeight and calculateTax), and are passing them into the calculateTotalCost function as an array argument. As you can see, it is no different than creating an array of any other type of object.

To reference a method without calling it, simply omit the braces.

```
console.log(calculateTax);
console.log(calculateTax({ price: 5.00 }));
```

The first line says "Show me what calculateTax is"; the second says "Execute calculateTax and give me the result". This gives us

```
[Function]
0.75
```

"this"

The keyword "this" will be well known to most developers since it exists in several languages. However, it can sometimes be frustrating to work with in JavaScript as it works according to different rules than it does elsewhere.

In JavaScript, the "this" keyword will normally point you to the object which called the current function, or the top level object (such as the browser window) if you are not in a function.

Unless it is called in a constructor function (more on which later), it which case it *will* give you the current instance.

This behaviour can cause a few headaches if you are not aware of it – for example, if you assume that "this" will behave as it does in other languages, always giving you the current instance.

Let's say we have the following code:

```
var Dog = function() {
    this.phrase = "Woof!";
    this.talk = function() {
            console.log(this.phrase);
    }
};

var dog = new Dog();
dog.talk();
```

This will cause the output:

[32]

```
Woof!
```

in the console. However, if we copy the function away from its object, like so:

```
var talk = dog.talk;
talk();
```

We get "undefined" instead. The calling context is now the top level object, rather than dog; since the top level element does not have a phrase property, this.phrase returns Undefined.

This is the same reason that the following two event handlers are not equivalent, even if in the end they are calling the same function:

```
$("#v1").click(dog.talk);
$("#v2").click(function() { dog.talk(); });
```

The first one results in "undefined", while the second one results in "Woof!". In the first case, we are effectively copying the function into the event handler, changing the context and giving a new meaning to "this". In the second one, we are only wrapping it, preserving the original context and letting it work normally.

Preserving context using closures

You may occasionally have come across a pattern which is commonly used to keep a reference to the instance which "owns" the function, making the state behave more like it would in other languages. This is done through a variable passed through a closure.

In most cases, these variables tend to be called "self" or some variation thereof, though this is only a convention. You could call it Susan, if it makes you happy – it would still work in the same way[5].

```
var Dog = function() {

    var self = this;

    this.phrase = "Woof!";
    this.talk = function() {
            console.log(self.phrase);
    }
};

var dog = new Dog();
var talk = dog.talk;
talk();
```

---

[5] If you are writing code for a living, don't call your variables Susan unless you have valid business reasons to do so.

This time, talk will result in "Woof!" being passed to the console, even if it was detached from the dog instance.

As we saw previously in the section on closures, the "talk" function scope keeps track of the "self" variable from its parent scope.

The advantage of this method is that it is self contained – as long as you use your "self" variable within your code, it doesn't really matter what you do to your functions outside of it.

Technically speaking, the example above where we used

```
$("#v2").click(function() { dog.talk(); });
```

is also making use of closures – in this case we're wrapping the function call and keeping the dog instance in scope. Personally I'm not really for this method as it's more verbose and someone will, sooner or later, forget to make a wrapper function leading to several hours of debugging.

Bind

A much preferable alternative is to use a function's Bind function. This lets you create a copy of the function with a definite context:

```
function greet() {
    console.log(this.name + ": " + this.phrase);
}
```

```
var talk1 = greet.bind({ name: "Dog", phrase:
"Hello? Yes, this is Dog." });
var talk2 = greet.bind({ name: "Sheep", phrase:
"Baaa!" });

talk1();
talk2();
```

This will write:

```
Dog: Hello? Yes, this is Dog.
Sheep: Baaa!
```

In this case, greet wasn't even inside either of the two objects to begin with; we can bind any function to any object, even one we made up on the spot, and it will become "this" for the function in question.

Bind returns a copy of the function, and doesn't affect the original. In this case, if we were to call greet, we'd only see

```
undefined: undefined
```

as "this" is unbound and would default to the root object.

The bind function also allows us to pre-set function arguments. For example:

```
function greet(adjective) {
```

```
    console.log(
            adjective + " " +
            this.name + ": " +
            this.phrase);
}

talk = greet.bind({
        name: "Dog",
        phrase: "Such bind. Many wow."
}, "Brown");

talk();
```

In this case, we would see

```
Brown Dog: Such bind. Many wow.
```

The adjective was set even though we called talk without any arguments, because we specified it in the binding call. If the function takes more than one parameter, you can add them as well; just call bind as if you were calling a function normally, adding your context before all the other parameters.

If you pre-set parameters in this way, parameters you pass in when calling the bound function will be ignored.

Callbacks

Callbacks are functions which are passed as arguments to other functions. This pattern is very common in most frameworks, especially when dealing with asynchronous behaviour.

The idea is for the main function to use the callback when something important happens. For example

```
var tick = function() {
    console.log("Tick!");
}
window.setTimeout(tick, 1000);
```

tells a browser to call the tick function when one second has elapsed. To give an example from the jQuery framework, the ajax function accepts callbacks for request completion and errors in communication. This allows you to specify what should happen next in either of these situations.

It is normal for callbacks to receive some information from the function which calls them – this will normally be documented.

When working with callbacks, it is important to remember that "this" will point to the object calling the function, not the object where the callback was defined. You may want to use one of the methods for preserving the context described above.

Object Oriented JavaScript

While you can write some useful scripts with functions alone, once your applications start growing in size and scope you're going to need to sort out your code to protect your scalp from deforestation.

Organizing your code into objects helps keep things clear and allows you a greater degree of reusability.

Even if you work on smaller scripts and rely on frameworks to do most of the heavy lifting, it helps to understand a little about object orientation, since most of them are heavily object based anyway.

At the simplest level, an object describes something in your application. Let's say a user. The user object might contain the user name and id, a function to get any messages they have, and a function to log them out. Any other functions you want to create that affect your user would go in there.

Now that you have a user object, you will want to keep it consistent across your application, so you create a User class. This will act as a template for all the instances of your user objects.

Classes also allow you to set up an object hierarchy through inheritance. Let's say that you have two types of user – a basic user and an administrative user. The administrative user class shares all the details in the basic user class, and adds some more on top.

You could of course copy the same functions from one class to the other, but that makes it hell to manage if you need to change any common code. Instead, you can declare that the administrative user class is based on the basic user class, so that it inherits all the common stuff.

In the following sections, we shall look at how we can create classes, objects, and work with class hierarchies.

Classes

Classes are essentially templates for objects in your script; they describe a set of properties and behaviours shared by objects of the same type.

In JavaScript, classes don't exist as independent entities; there is no class statement or class type. Instead, functions take over this role; the class of an object is determined by the constructor used to construct it.

We shall continue to refer to classes as "classes", simply because that is what they logically *are* even if there is no other distinguishing feature from other functions. If one is used to OOP terms, it is easier to understand this way.

Constructors

In JavaScript, constructors are simply functions which set the initial state of an object. There is no deep magic to worry about.

Inside a constructor, "this" will refer to the new object being created as long as you have called the function with the "new" keyword. Constructors can be as simple as empty functions:

```
var Dog = function() {
}
```

You may of course add any initialisation you like in there.

Creating instances

Once you have your constructor set up, you can create a new instance by calling it with the "new" keyword:

```
var dog = new Dog();
```

This implicitly create an object, and run the constructor function on it – in the constructor, "this" will be referring to the newly created object. The following is an approximation of what is going on here:

```
var dog = {};
dog.constructor = Dog;
dog.constructor();
```

Once the constructor has been called, your object instance is ready for use.

"Singleton" constructors

Instead of creating a constructor function and creating a new object, sometimes you may just call "new" directly on the function declaration, like so:

```
var Messages = new function() {

    this.messages = [];

    this.hasMessages = function() {
            return this.messages.length > 0;
```

```
        }

    this.add = function(message) {
        this.messages.push(message);
    }

    this.show = function() {

        if (!this.hasMessages()) {
            console.log("== No messages ==");
            return;
        }

        for (var i = 0;
            i < this.messages.length; i++) {
            console.log(this.messages[i]);
        }
    }
}

Messages.show();

Messages.add("Hi!");
Messages.add("Another message");
Messages.show();
```

You will find this useful when you have an object which you will only ever need one instance of in your application. For example, here we're defining a class which will manage notifications for the user. We'll only need one of these in the application, since we want all the messages to go through here.

[43]

This means that having a separate constructor isn't particularly useful, and may actually be counterproductive since someone may[6] accidentally create a new instance. That would leave us wondering why our nice messaging system is only working around half the time.

By calling new directly on the constructor declaration, we're creating a new object immediately, without leaving a reference constructor function lying around. The Messages variable will be assigned an object – in the example, you can see that we are making calls on it – rather than a function.

This pattern can be used to mimic the singleton pattern in other languages.

Of course, we could always forego the constructor function and create the object inline, which is something we shall look at later.

---

[6] "May" tends towards "will" as the number of people involved in a project approaches 1 or higher and time is greater than 0.

Objects

Objects are specific instances of a class, and are implemented as hashes. Among other things, this means you can access their properties and functions using either the "." notation, as we have been doing in most of these examples, or the array notation:

```
var Rabbit = function(colour) {
    this.colour = colour;
}


var rabbit = new Rabbit("white");
console.log(rabbit.colour);
console.log(rabbit["colour"]);
```

Both the logs above will access the "colour" property of the rabbit instance.

In general you will not need to use the array notation; it is most useful when the property or function which you need to pick in a particular script is not pre-determined.

In the example below, we will pick a property based on an argument we pass to a function, and display the named property:

```
var Rabbit = function(colour, hasWatch) {
    this.colour = colour;
    this.hasWatch = hasWatch;
}
```

```
var LogRabbitProperty = function(rabbit,
propertyId) {

    var propertyName = (propertyId === 0)
        ? "colour"
        : "hasWatch"

    console.log(propertyName + ": " +
rabbit[propertyName]);
}

var rabbit = new Rabbit("white", true);
LogRabbitProperty(rabbit, 0);
LogRabbitProperty(rabbit, 1);
```

If you are using this method, you may of course use whatever way you need to get to the names.

Adding Properties or Functions to Objects

JavaScript isn't terribly particular about sticking to classes; it will cheerfully allow you to add members to instances ad hoc. In fact you will find yourself doing this quite often.

Assigning a member to an object works in exactly the same way as assigning a variable; you only need to prefix your member name with the name of the object, for example:

```
rabbit.isLate = true;
```

Note that in this case, we do not use the var keyword. The variable – in this case, rabbit – is already defined, so we just want to add stuff on top of it.

When assigning properties or functions to an object, both notations add to the same place, so it doesn't matter which notation you use to add a property for example; it can be read back in either notation:

```
rabbit.isLate = true;
console.log(rabbit["isLate"]);

rabbit["isRunning"] = true;
console.log(rabbit.isRunning);
```

Both of these will display their value correctly.

The exception to this is, if you use the array notation to add a name which is not a valid JavaScript identifier, then you will only be able to access it using the array notation; trying to call it via the dot notation will just cause a syntax error:

```
rabbit["Got a vicious streak a mile wide"] =
false;
console.log(rabbit["Got a vicious streak a mile
wide"]);
console.log(rabbit.Got a vicious streak a mile
wide);
```

The first accessor should work fine, but the second one will fail because you can't have spaces in your identifiers.

Using property names like this is one of those things which you *can* do, but perhaps should not. I can't recall any cases where I *needed* to use this pattern, and although they may exist, my advice would be to have a good think about it before you implement something in this way as it is becomes quite counter-intuitive.

In general, if you already have a class structure and you find yourself adding the same things over again, it makes most sense to use the prototype function to attach members to the class. In this way, all objects of the same class will have access to them.

Namespaces

If you have done much non-JavaScript programming, you may be familiar with the concept of namespacing – organizing classes in modules or packages to keep some semblance of sanity in your pile of code.

JavaScript supports namespacing implicitly. That is to say, there isn't a specific namespace keyword; you can simply use an object as a namespace.

Let's say we have some of geometry classes in our script:

```
var Geometry = new function() {
    this.G2D = new function() {
        this.Point = function(x, y) {
```

```
                    this.x = x;
                    this.y = y;

                    this.DistanceFrom =
function(point) {

                        var dX = this.x - point.x;
                        var dY = this.y - point.y;

                        return Math.sqrt(
                            (dX * dX) +
                            (dY * dY) );
                    }
                };
            };
        };
```

Here we're using a singleton constructor to create an object called Geometry, and a second one to create an object called G2D inside it (for 2D Geometry – identifiers cannot start with a number).

This lets us call our Point class like so:

```
var pointA = new Geometry.G2D.Point(0,0);
var pointB = new Geometry.G2D.Point(2,2);

console.log(pointA.DistanceFrom(pointB));
```

This is particularly useful in conjunction with a good file structure; once you start splitting up your scripts into files, it's a good idea to namespace so you know what file to look in. In this example, it might make sense for the Geometry namespace to be defined in a file called geometry.js

Since namespaces are still plain old objects, you can always add more stuff to them. Say we add some 3D geometry – maybe in a file called g3d.js

```
Geometry.G3D = new function() {
    this.Point = function(x, y, z) {

        this.x = x;
        this.y = y;
        this.z = z;

        this.DistanceFrom = function(point) {

            var dX = this.x - point.x;
            var dY = this.y - point.y;
            var dZ = this.z - point.z;

            return Math.sqrt(
                (dX * dX) +
                (dY * dY) +
                (dZ * dZ));
        }
    }
};
```

This will add the G3D namespace to the Geometry namespace, so we can now use 3d points:

```
var pointA = new Geometry.G3D.Point(0,0,0);
var pointB = new Geometry.G3D.Point(2,2,2);


console.log(pointA.DistanceFrom(pointB));
```

Now, this example would fail if we hadn't previously loaded the geometry.js file. In most places where you would use this pattern, you would want to check that the parent namespace exists before you assign to it.

Let's clean up our example. First, we split it into two files – maybe we can put them in a folder called geometry to keep things organized. Now we have

geometry/g2d.js
geometry/g3d.js

Now, at the beginning of each file, we can add a check:

```
if (!Geometry) Geometry = {};
Geometry.G2D = new function() { ...
```

```
if (!Geometry) Geometry = {};
Geometry.G3D = new function() { ...
```

Each file only worries about its own namespace. If the geometry namespace has not been created when the file loads, it will get created immediately, otherwise, we simply add to what is already there.

Prototypes

Now, although JavaScript is fully object oriented the flexible nature of its classes means that some things work in a slightly different way than they do in languages such as Java.

JavaScript is prototype based, which means that you can use your objects as templates (or indeed prototypes) for other classes. This is almost identical to the way inheritance works in most object oriented languages:

```
var Animal = function() {
    this.talk = function() {
            console.log(this.phrase);
    }
}

var Dog = function() {
    Animal.call();
    this.phrase = "Woof!";
}

var Sheep = function() {
    Animal.call();
    this.phrase = "Baa!";
}

Dog.prototype = new Animal();
Sheep.prototype = new Animal();

var charlie = new Dog();
var itchy = new Dog();
```

```
var aSheep = new Sheep();

charlie.talk();
itchy.talk();
aSheep.talk();
```

This will log:

```
Woof!
Woof!
Baa!
```

In this case, both the sheep and the dog class have access to the talk function defined in Animal, as we have declared the prototype for both to be Animal.

Note the call function in both the subclasses. While in this case it is not necessary, it may be used to pass any arguments needed by the parent class.

Once a prototype is assigned, any changes in the class are reflected in all instances of the class, including ones which have been created already. If we were to add the following to our example:

```
Dog.prototype.wag = function(number) {

    var message = "";

    for (var i = 0; i < number; i++) {
```

```
        message += "Wag";
    }

    console.log(message);
}

charlie.wag(3);
itchy.wag(2);
```

In this case both instances of Dog would have access to the wag function. This is different from assigning the function directly to an object – if instead of using prototype, we said

```
charlie.wag = function(number) ...
```

Then only that *specific* instance would have had access to the wag method.

The Constructor property

With objects, typeof will always evaluate to "object". This makes it less than useful to determine what class we are dealing with.

We can get some more information using the constructor property, which will give us the constructor which was used in the object's creation. This can be compared to the class constructor,

Unfortunately, it will give us the top level constructor, so if we refer back to the previous example,

```
itchy.constructor === Dog
```

would evaluate to false, since Dog itself is derived from Animal... unless we take a small extra step when assigning the prototype:

```
Dog.prototype = new Animal();
Dog.prototype.constructor = Dog;
```

In this case, the constructor property for instances of Dog would return the Dog constructor, allowing you to test for class.

Inline Definitions and JSON

In the last few years, JSON (JavaScript object notation) has gained a lot of traction as a data interchange format. It has a number of advantages – it's compact, and natively readable by JavaScript, since it essentially is JavaScript.

Consider the following piece of JSON:

```
{
    name: "karl",
    id: 1278
}
```

If you have been paying attention to the previous examples, the format should be familiar. We've been using it all along to define inline objects. In fact, JSON objects are nothing more than plain old JavaScript objects defined using the inline notation.

Inlining is not limited to data interchange of course; you can use it as part of your own scripts to declare your objects, particularly if you do not need to keep a constructor.

If we go back to the singleton class example, we could rewrite it to use inline declarations as follows:

```
var Messages = {

    messages: [],
```

```javascript
    hasMessages: function() {
        return this.messages.length > 0;
    },

    add: function(message) {
        this.messages.push(message);
    },

    show: function() {

        if (!this.hasMessages()) {
            console.log("== No messages ==");
            return;
        }

        for (var i = 0;
            i < this.messages.length; i++) {
            console.log(this.messages[i]);
        }
    }
};
```

In this case, note how the members are declared using the form [identifier: value], rather than [identifier = value]. Also notice how within the object, the declarations are delimited by a comma, rather than a semicolon; while we are in the object description, we are still in the same statement.

When we use the form

```javascript
var x = {}
```

we are essentially saying

```
var x = new Object();
```

This creates an empty instance of the object class, to which we can add further members.

If you look at the messages property, you will also see that we are initializing an array in the same way:

```
messages: []
```

This is shorthand for

```
messages: new Array()
```

As with the inline declaration of objects, you can also add values to an array as you initialize it inline:

```
messages: ["Hi!", "This message will be in the
array"]
```

This form of initialization is useful when you need to pass an object argument to a function, as you can just generate it on the spot without having to worry about making a constructor and such.

Strict Mode JavaScript

JavaScript is generally quite lenient as a language. As we have already seen, it tends to let quite a lot slide. This sometimes becomes a problem, particularly in larger applications, as some things may not quite work the way you intended due to some subtle difference in the way you expressed yourself at some point.

JavaScript engines which support ECMAScript 5 or higher[7] provide a mechanism to allow you to opt in for strict mode. This causes the scripts to be interpreted in a slightly different way. In many cases, this results in exceptions being thrown when you do something which looks ambiguous.

The idea is to standardize the behaviour of the script, making it more predictable – this leads to fewer surprises down the road. For the sake of future compatibility, most manufacturers recommend using strict mode as much as possible, as it is likely that the JavaScript specification will tend in this direction in future.

Enabling Strict Mode

To enable strict mode, simply put the following statement at the beginning of your file or function:

---

[7] At the time of writing, most major browsers support this. In the case of Internet Explorer, Strict mode is supported from IE10 upwards.

```
"use strict";
```

This statement has to appear before any other statement in the file or function, otherwise it will be ignored.

This may be a problem if you concatenate your files, as you may find yourself in a situation where all your scripts are treated as strict (because the first file is strict) or all your script is treated as non-strict (because the first file isn't strict).

In these situations, you might want consider concatenating files separately, or using function-level strict mode to prevent confusion.

Effects of Strict Mode

Strict mode changes quite a number of things, some of which are well beyond the scope of this book. Let's look at changes which affect things we have already looked at.

In strict mode, it is no longer possible to declare variables implicitly. The following:

```
"use strict";
fail = "Hi!";
```

will result in an error as fail is not defined as a variable before we try to assign to it. This helps avoid problems when you mistype the name of the variable (I'm reliably assured that it happens to some people), or when you try to assign to a variable which is not available in the current scope.

This also happens if you try to do something which would, in non-strict mode, result in a silent failure. For example, if we were to try to mess around with a property which is non-assignable:

```
"use strict";
Object.prototype = function() {
    console.log("o hai!");
}
```

In non-strict mode, that will do absolutely nothing; Object.property won't be affected because it's a read only property, but nothing will tell us that. Strict mode, on the other hand, will immediately let us know when we try to poke something which we shouldn't:

```
TypeError: Cannot assign to read only property
'prototype' of function Object()
```

Strict mode also stops you from declaring functions anywhere except the top level of your script or function. In other words, this:

```
"use strict";
var x = 0;
if (x == 0) {
```

```
function func() {
        console.log("X is greater than 1");


    }
}
```

Will fail with the exception:

```
SyntaxError: In strict mode code, functions can
only be declared at top level or immediately
within another function.
```

I'm not quite sure why anyone would want to do that in the first place, as it's terribly counterintuitive to me, but apparently it was enough of a problem that someone decided to explicitly disallow it.

You can of course still declare functions within functions.

Finally (as far as this overview is concerned) the following words *may not* be used as identifiers as they are reserved for possible future use:

- implements
- interface
- let
- package
- private

- protected
- public
- static
- yield

Since it is possible that any or all of these words will be used as keywords in future versions of JavaScript, avoiding their use now will save you from having to hunt them down and changing them later.

For a complete overview of all changes under strict mode, you can refer to document ECMAScript Language Specification 5.1 edition (ECMA-262), which can be downloaded from the ECMA site (http://www.ecma-international.org/)

Index

P

Parameters · 20
   By Reference · 24
   By Value · 23
   Optional · 21
Prototypes · 53
   prototype (Function) · 53

R

Return · 26
   Multiple · 27
   Undefined · 28

S

Scope · 12

Separation of Concerns · 26
Strict Mode · 60

T

this (keyword) · 32
typeof · 3, 55

U

Undefined · 3

V

var · 2, 14

I hope that this brief overview of these features and patterns proves useful in your work and helps clear up some doubts or questions you may have had about these aspects of the language.

While every effort has been made to make sure that the information in this text is correct, I'm sure at least something slipped through the net, so if you spot any glaring inaccuracies, by all means please contact me on my blog (link below).

On that note, I would like to thank Claire Graf, David Bonnici, Matthew Sant and Chris Cachia Zammit for reviewing the text and pointing out the cases of teh stupidz which crept in during the writing. Any that remain are entirely my bad.

Good luck, and good coding.

Karl lives in (at the time of writing) face-meltingly hot Malta, and has worked in software development for longer than most decent people would be willing to remind him.

When he is not commanding machines to do his bidding, he studies sword fighting and updates his blog at http://karlagius.com whenever it occurs to him to do so, which is really not very often.